THIS BOOK is to
commemorate the issuance of the
Pure Silver Yakima medal
December 31, 1972
and is limited to 15,000 copies

No. _10225_

Photograph by Richard D. Daughe
MT. ADAMS, seen from the Yakima Summer gathering camp at Potato Hill.

THE
YAKIMA
PEOPLE

by Dr. Richard D. Daugherty

Scientific Editors: Henry F. Dobyns & Robert C. Euler
General Editor: John I. Griffin

PUBLISHED BY INDIAN TRIBAL SERIES / PHOENIX

ABOUT THE TRIBAL CHAIRMAN

ROBERT B. JIM, Chairman of the Yakima Tribal Council, was born June 28, 1929, at Dry Creek, Washington. He attended public schools in Toppenish, Washington, graduating in 1948. He enlisted that fall in the United States Air Force and served in France, Germany and England until he was discharged with rank of staff sargeant in April, 1954. Mr. Jim then returned to Dry Creek, where he chased wild horses, lived and hunted in the mountains, and fished at the ancient historical fishing site at Celilo, Oregon, until it was inundated in 1957.

Mr. Jim joined the Yakima Tribal Council in November of 1957. In 1961, he served as treasurer of the National Congress of American Indians. In 1962, he was Commander of the Chief White Swan Post No. 191 of the American Legion, Secretary of the Affiliated Tribes of Northwest Indians, and became Chairman of the American Indian Civil Liberties Trust. Two years later, Mr. Jim was appointed for a 21-year term on the Trust, and journeyed to Quito, Ecuador, as a member of the United States delegation to the Interamerican Indian Congress.

Named Chairman of the Yakima Tribal Council in 1967, Mr. Jim joined the Board of Directors of the National Tribal Chairman's Association in 1972. President Richard M. Nixon appointed Mr. Jim to the National Council of Indian Opportunity for a term ending on August 31, 1974.

The Chairman is married to Ernestine A. Jim of Wapato, Washington. They have four sons and three daughters.

Chairman Jim and his people are proud not only of recovering Mount Adams, but also of their efforts on behalf of their fellow native Americans. They helped Taos Pueblo of New Mexico by inviting Taos to ceremonies initiating Senator Henry M. Jackson as a member of the Yakima Tribe in 1970, when he was given an Indian name. They were able thus to acquaint the Taos with a key senator for the passage of legislation the Taos sought for 60 years to regain their sacred Blue Lake.

The Yakima under Chairman Jim were able to aid the Alaskan Federation of Natives when their resources were exhausted and they were advised to settle for 7,000,000 acres and a few million dollars. The Yakima Tribe loaned the AFN $225,000 in August, 1970. In December of 1971 the Alaskan natives finally secured a settlement for 40,000,000 acres of land and one billion dollars.

BERT B. JIM, Chairman of the Yakima Tribal Council.

Photograph by Harvey S. Rice, Washington Archaeological Research Cen
MODERN DIPNET FISHING on the Klickitat River.

THE CONFEDERATED TRIBES and Bands of the Yakima Nation once occupied nearly seventeen thousand square miles of land in the western part of the American Plateau. Their territory extended from the glaciated summits and forested slopes of the Cascade Mountains on the west to the open sagebrush desert and rocky basalt canyons of the Columbia Basin on the east. Named for one of the 14 tribes and bands that signed the Treaty of 1855, this confederated group includes speakers of three language families, Sahaptian, Salishan, and Chinookan.

Lying between the Cascade and the Rocky Mountains, and extending from the great bend of the Fraser River in British Columbia to northern Oregon, is the culture area known to ethnographers as the Plateau. Within this vast geographical region lie the territories of many

1

peoples possessing a similar way of life, at least more similar one to the other than each is to groups in the neighboring culture areas of the Northwest Coast to the west, the Great Basin on the south, the Plains to the east, or the Athapascan culture area to the north. The Plateau Culture Area sometimes is divided on cultural grounds into a northern section, the Canadian Plateau, and the southern or American Plateau section.

The lands of the Yakima offered many and varied resources to these people who secured their livelihood by fishing, hunting, and gathering wild plant foods, and also a wide variety of local environments through which to range as they followed their seasonal economic round. Although the prehistoric Yakima were no doubt aware that crops were being cultivated by other native American groups who lived great distances away, they never adopted any form of agriculture prior to their direct contact with Euro-American culture at the beginning of the nineteenth century. They preferred, instead, to utilize the rich resources that their environment had to offer, particularly the migrating runs of salmon that filled their rivers and tributary streams during certain seasons of the year.

ORIGINS

Evidence of the earliest human populations to occupy the lands of the Yakima has yet to be discovered. Archaeological research has revealed, nonetheless, that shortly after the last of the Pleistocene glaciers began to recede about 14,000 years ago, nomadic bands possessing a well-developed technology for the manufacture of stone and bone tools were roaming over the area hunting large and small game, fishing for salmon, collecting river mussels, and gathering wild plant foods. The stone and bone working technology which was so highly developed at this early time, as developed as it ever was to become in an area that is noted for the sophistication of its stone artifacts, indicates that thousands of years of cultural development preceded those early cultures — either here or elsewhere in the New World.

Yakima prehistory can be divided conveniently into five main periods: the *Early Period* (before 9,000 years ago), the *Transitional Period* (from 9,000 to 4,500 years ago), the *Developmental Period* (from 4,500 years ago to 0-BC/AD), the *Climax Period* (from 0-BC/AD to 1805 AD), and the *Historic Period* (post 1805 AD).

The climate of the Early Period during the first few thousand years following the Pleistocene glaciers was cooler and more moist than the climate of today. The desert areas in the eastern part of Yakima territory were dotted with lakes and drained by numerous small streams. Grasslands with scattered stands of pine

3

and willow trees grew where sagebrush now flourishes. The animals present included all of the modern species plus some large forms that are now extinct. A giant form of bison was being hunted by man. Although numerous remains of mammoths and the scattered bones of other extinct forms such as horses have been discovered, none of these has been found in a context indicating that they were being hunted for food. This is rather curious because elsewhere in North America a number of kill sites have been found showing that man was hunting mammoths with some considerable success. In the Pacific Northwest we have either failed to find evidence of this or else the prehistoric residents displayed a distinct preference for other game.

The way of life of these early people may be learned from examining the types of artifacts and other kinds of evidence that have been excavated from their campsites. It must be remembered that as non-agricultural peoples they, as well as those who followed them in time, had a definite seasonal round of economic activities. At any one archaeological site we may be catching only the briefest glimpse of but one phase of this economic cycle.

Ten to 12,000 years ago small bands, or perhaps extended family groups, periodically camped at the Lind Coulee Site which was situated on a sluggish stream or lake in the eastern part of Yakima country. They came there to hunt large game including bison, antelope, deer, and smaller animals such as foxes, muskrats, and rabbits. They also hunted ducks and geese and gathered eggs from the nests. Turtles were caught and eaten. It is likely that they also were gathering wild plant foods and perhaps were doing some fishing as well, but if so, evidence of these activities has not survived.

The abundant animal bones found in the site deposits, particularly those of the giant bison, indicate that they were skilled hunters. The stemmed stone projectile points, probably fastened to a short spear that was thrown with the aid of a spear thrower, were beautifully made. The broad, flat thinning flakes that had been skillfully and symmetrically removed in the shaping of these points indicate that the makers had a great deal of knowledge about stone flaking techniques as well as considerable control in the execution of their craft. Two bone points were found that had serrated notches cut along one side, and may have been used in the taking of waterfowl. The recovery of a number of stone scraping tools suggests that the dressing of hides for use as clothing may well have been an important activity at the site. Another activity was the preparation of red and yellow pigment for use as paint, probably for personal adornment and perhaps associated in part with

5

certain ceremonial activities. This pigment could have been used also for painting their tools, weapons, and perhaps skin containers. Its abundance in the deposits, plus the discovery of a stone palette on which the pigment had been ground, indicates that it was frequently used.

Another early archaeological site sheds additional light on the economic activities and way of life during early postglacial times. On the Oregon side of the Columbia River near The Dalles, just across the river from historic Yakima territory, a site was discovered and excavated that contained, among other things, tens of thousands of salmon vertebrae. Known as the Roadcut Site at Five Mile Rapids, this site is near the historic salmon fishery of Celilo Falls, and indicates that nearly 10,000 years ago, as well as in historic times, the taking of salmon was a very important economic activity.

As with the people who periodically occupied the Lind Coulee Site, the people who lived here had a rich bone tool industry and in addition a considerable number of tools made of antler. Although fishing appears to have been the principal economic activity at Five Mile Rapids, the large and varied animal assemblage recovered in the excavations tells us that hunting, particularly the hunting of birds, also was important. The variety of birds represented, including among others, cormorants, geese, condors, turkey vultures, and eagles, suggests that at least

Photograph by Richard D. Daugherty

CAVATORS UNEARTHING a giant elk, a type now extinct, which was killed and
en 10,000 years ago by inhabitants of Marmes Rockshelter.

some of these species were being hunted for their feathers. This, along with the abundance of red pigment here also provides fair evidence of a concern for personal adornment, and perhaps even evidence for the existence of ceremonial garb.

Near the confluence of the Palouse and Snake Rivers, in the extreme southeastern part of Yakima territory, yet another early archaeological site has been excavated which is providing us with new insights into the lives of the people who lived here following the retreat of the last glaciers. Known as Marmes Rockshelter, this small, cavelike opening in the basalt cliffs contained many feet of stratified cultural deposits rich in artifacts representing ten millenia of human activities. The deposits also contained 24 human burials, nine of which date from approximately 10,000 years ago. Of particular interest is the fact that most, if not all of these earliest burials had been cremated. This represents the earliest record of this type of funeral practice in the Western Hemisphere if not in the world. Careful study of the bones has indicated that the population of 10,000 years ago was fully modern in physical appearance.

Marmes Rockshelter appears to have been used at times as a temporary campsite and at other times as a place for the disposal of the dead. The faunal remains indicate that the hunting of deer, antelope, and elk was being carried on with considerable success, while fishing appears to have been a rather unimportant activity at this locality.

The earliest known peoples of the New World are often portrayed as being primarily hunters of big game animals, because little evidence exists of other kinds of economic activities. Marmes Rockshelter provides such evidence. Here four grinding stones with shallow depressions worn in their surfaces were recovered from the earliest deposits, plus quantities of chokecherry pits. The early people of our area definitely gathered and processed wild plant foods.

One artifact discovered in the earliest levels at Marmes Rockshelter is of considerable importance because of its very small size. This is a perfectly made, tiny bone needle no larger than the average size steel needle found in a modern sewing basket. The implication derived from this discovery is that these people were sewing tailored skin garments with watertight seams to enable them to withstand the cold and wet weather of the early postglacial period.

In summary, the evidence indicates that the people who lived in Yakima territory prior to 9,000 years ago were physically fully modern. They possessed technological skills which enabled them to flake stone tools as well as they were able to do in the succeeding 9,000 years.

9

They also fashioned well-made tools of bone and antler, and prepared animal skins and sewed them into finely made tailored garments.

They successfully hunted large and small game animals and birds, and had developed very adequate techniques for the taking of salmon and other fish. By this time, also, they were using grinding stones in the preparation of their vegetable foods. Finally, the abundant occurrence of red pigment plus the likelihood that some of the birds hunted were being sought for their feathers, indicates a concern for personal adornment.

Lacking in the archaeological inventories from the Early Period is any evidence about types of houses that were in use. Although it is likely that these were aboveground structures with a framework of poles covered by brush or matting, specific evidence of this is still to be found. Also missing is any indication that these people wove baskets and mats of vegetable fibres. Again, it is highly likely that they did, but no fragments of baskets or mats, highly perishable types of artifacts, have survived the destructive forces of nature for 9,000 or more years.

The basic technologies and the basic patterns of economic life of the historic Yakima had already been developed by the end of the Early Period, 9,000 years ago.

The Transitional Period, lasting from the end

10

of the Early Period until approximately 4,500 years ago, is so named because unlike the period before and that which followed, this one cannot be characterized as one during which significant technological advances were made, when the methods of exploiting any of the food resources were improved, or during which the pattern of living was changed in any recognizable way. Nor was this a period of cultural regression. It appears, simply, as if the adjustments that had to be made to the rather pronounced climatic changes that occurred during this time fully captured people's attention and energies.

One of the hallmarks of the prehistoric cultural development in the intermontane region of the Pacific Northwest is that of cultural conservatism, which is characterized by cultural change that took place slowly and without dramatic alteration in pace or content. Much of the evidence of cultural change to be seen in the archaeological record exists in the form of stylistic variations in basic artifact forms and occasionally the addition of a new artifact type or technological process. Certainly by any measure, the Transitional was a conservative period with only modest change.

The Transitional Period closely approximates in time the warm, dry, Altithermal climatic episode of the postglacial period. As we have seen earlier the climate of the Early Period was cooler and more moist than is the present day

11

climate of this region. Climatic conditions were ameliorating, and by about 9,000 years ago the climate was again about as it is today. This warming and drying trend continued, however, and by around 6,500 years ago the climate was considerably warmer and drier than at present. Pronounced environmental changes no doubt accompanied this alteration in climate, introducing changes in vegetation and fauna, dropping the flow of major rivers to a very low level, and completely drying up some of the smaller lakes and streams.

About 7,000 years ago, just before the peak of this warming trend, a series of convulsive volcanic explosions blew the top off a mountain in the Cascade Range of southern Oregon, blanketing the Pacific Northwest with volcanic ash, and creating the beautiful Crater Lake of today. Geologists refer to this now nonexistent peak as Mt. Mazama. Volcanic ash is composed primarily of tiny glass fragments, and we can only speculate as to the effect of this ash fall on the grazing and browsing animals from ingesting quantities of this material along with their food. It may well have produced a temporary decline in the number of animals available for food.

The basic way of human life, however, continued through the Transitional Period. That some economic adjustments were made in response to the changing climate is becoming increasingly clear from the archaeological record. It has been suggested that the extremely arid conditions of the desert regions would have forced abandonment of this part of Yakima territory until climatic conditions moderated. Yet archaeological evidence indicates that at least along the Snake and Columbia rivers many sites were being occupied at this time. It can be seen, however, that the numbers of antelope bones found in refuse heaps increased with a corresponding drop in the number of deer and elk bones. The numbers of food grinding implements also increased dramatically.

Many more archaeological sites dating from the Transitional Period are known than are recorded from the preceding period. This not only reflects better archaeological preservation but probably indicates also an expanding population. Of considerable interest is the fact that although the styles of stone projectile points changed significantly, they were being manufactured by utilizing the same distinctive stone-flaking technology that characterized the preceding period.

It appears evident that the Transitional Period cultures developed primarily out of the local cultures of the preceding Early Period with little external influence. For the first time, however, evidence of trade relations with coastal areas now begins to appear in the form of numerous *Olivella* shell beads. Also artifact assemblages somewhat resembling those of Transitional

Period sites of the interior have been found in archaeological sites of the same time period close to Puget Sound in western Washington suggesting at least some limited cultural contact between peoples of the interior and those of the coast.

In the latter part of the Transitional Period, following the Mazama ash fall, a new projectile point style was introduced. This is a large, side-notched point that is found at about this same time over wide areas of North America. Whether or not this represents some additional outside cultural influence, perhaps from the northeastern Great Basin area of southern Idaho where similar projectile points occur at a slightly earlier time, is not clear at present.

In summary, the Transitional Period is characterized by continuity of the life style developed in the preceding period, by continuity in the technology employed in the manufacture of stone tools, by continuity of most of the basic artifacts, but by stylistic changes in the form of a number of these artifact types. It is characterized by an expanding population and expanding trade and perhaps somewhat broader cultural relationships with neighboring regions. That the cultural changes were not greater testifies to the varied and abundant resources of the region and the fact that man had learned to exploit most of these so that when times of economic stress occurred he was able to adjust

14

his economic life without having to make fundamental changes in this culture.

During the Developmental Period, which lasted from about 4,500 years ago until around the beginning of the Christian Era, the basic life-way of the prehistoric Yakima became fully established. It has been seen that the basic technologies for the manufacture of tools, weapons, and clothing had already been developed in the preceding periods, and that during these earlier periods adequate techniques had been arrived at for exploiting the food resources which their environment had to offer. What then was left to be "developed" during the Developmental Period?

The Developmental Period ushered in new stone-working technologies, no more efficient than those employed during the preceding period, simply different. It also had its characteristic projectile point styles. One new and significant addition to the artifact inventory was the ground stone adze blade made of nephrite or serpentine used in heavy woodworking. Because the source of this stone material, and probably the finished adzes themselves, lies in British Columbia, here is evidence of trade relationships to the north as well as the development of a woodworking industry.

Perhaps the most significant development that was taking place, however, was the gradual emergence of sizable winter villages located in strategic areas in the river valleys, areas that would provide warmer winter temperatures because of their lower elevation, fuel and fresh drinking water, and protection from the bitter winds of winter.

There obviously was no magic moment when these prehistoric residents decided to form large winter communities, when it was decided that their food storage capabilities were sufficient to support a large population through the season of lowest economic productivity, or when it was recognized that a larger population would permit greater social and ceremonial activity.

In the prehistoric record, it is clear that large winter villages are related to a continually increasing population which in turn may be related to more efficient economic activities — more efficient, but not different. It is unlikely that the hunting of game animals or the gathering of wild plant foods could be made much more efficient. This leaves only a change in the efficiency of fishing techniques as a likely possibility. As far as we know, there were countless thousands of salmon in the rivers which, if they could be caught in great numbers and properly dried and preserved and used in conjunction with other foods, would support a sizable population through the winter months.

It has been suggested that the development of fish traps and weirs, much more productive forms of fishing than the use of lines, spears, dipnets, or bows and arrows, led to a more dependable and substantial economic base and therefore to a rapidly expanding population. Evidence of large winter village communities exists in the form of extensive archaeological sites plus a new form of housing, the semisubterranean dwelling. Semisubterranean dwellings or "pit houses" as they are often called are structures erected over an excavated pit. In some areas of the Americas these structures take the form of semisubterranean earth lodges in which case, after a superstructure of poles and logs has been erected and covered with mats and grass or brush, the entire house, save for the above ground opening at the side or top, is covered with an insulating layer of earth. Not all semisubterranean houses were earth covered, however, and those found in Yakima territory were mostly of another type – a type with a long history among the prehistoric Yakima. Basic to this form of house is a tipilike framework of radiating poles covered with brush or mats. In summertime a single layer of mats, perhaps rolled up around the bottom for ventilation during the heat of the day, would provide shade from sun, protection from the winds, and shelter from an occasional thundershower. In the winter, multiple layers of mats would be secured to the framework for insulation from the cold. These mats froze and swelled in winter, keeping the wind and weather out. Icy winds would also be prevented from blowing through the house by piling up a few inches of earth around the bottom of the outside walls. As the weather became warmer, the roof mats dried and shrunk allowing household ventilation.

The size of this type of house was obviously limited by the length of the poles used, which was in turn limited by the size of trees locally available and, in the pre-horse era, by man's ability conveniently to move the poles from where they were cut to the village location. The diameter of such a house could be increased by spreading the base of the poles and thereby sacrificing the height of the ceiling, but this is not too successful an approach because the area close to the walls soon becomes unusable. One very satisfactory solution is to construct the house over a pit a few feet deep. In well-drained soil, this would provide a very snug winter dwelling, and permit the construction of circular houses thirty or more feet in diameter with adequater ceiling height even close to the walls. Semisubterranean houses of this size are commonly encountered in archaeological investigations. It is not known just how early in time the prehistoric Yakima used such structures, but radiocarbon dates on charcoal taken from hearths on the floors indicate that this form of house was being lived in prior to 3,000 years ago.

The circular mat-covered structure, whether

constructed over a pit or not, appears to be the basic structural unit from which later types of aboriginal housing developed. The elongated A-frame mat lodges of the protohistoric and early historic periods were simply a stretched version of the circular mat lodge. The skin covered tipi of the later periods involved replacing the mat covering with a new type of material and some subtle changes in the placement of the poles and interior structure, traits undoubtedly introduced from the Great Plains.

Certainly, well before the end of the Developmental Period large winter village settlements existed, usually located in the river valleys, often close to favored fishing sites. These larger winter settlements no doubt contributed to expanding wintertime social activities, and may well have ushered in the development of the winter ceremonial pattern.

The Climax Period (0-BC/AD to 1805 AD) is characterized by elaboration of economic and other social patterns that had already been established by the end of the preceding period. In particular, it can be seen that the population continued to expand, that trade relations with the Northwest coast, Plains, and Great Basin tribes increased considerably, and that an increased emphasis was being placed upon social and ceremonial activities.

Toward the end of the Climax Period, but well in advance of direct historical contact in the

WANAPAM VILLAGE AT PRIEST RAPIDS on the the Columbia River, built of elonga

A-frame mat-covered houses.

Pacific Northwest, the Yakima acquired the horse. The use of horses was quickly woven into the fabric of Yakima culture, permitting increased mobility, broader and stronger trade relationships, and heavier utilization of their economic resources. For not only was it easier to move about in their territory, but of greater importance was the fact that with horses they could carry quantities of food back to storage areas near the winter village. Along with the horse came a number of traits usually associated with the mounted bison-hunting tribes of the northern Plains. The traits included the paraphernalia associated with horses such as saddles, bridles, and quirts, patterns of dress and dress ornamentation, including feathered headdresses, but most important, ideas about tribal organization and warfare. These ideas, however, never fully replaced the earlier patterns of band organization and pacifism. Artifacts from archaeological sites dating from the Climax Period show an increase in the variety of implements employed in the same basic tasks. For instance, toggling harpoons and leisters have now been added to the inventory of fishing devices, and net gauges give the first definite indication of the use of fish nets. The new fishing traits along with clubs carved from whale bone may indicate closer and more prolonged contact with coastal tribes.

Improvements in the techniques for processing vegetable foods may be noted by the occurrence now of bowl-shaped mortars and elongate pestles.

Woodworking is seen to have become more important because serpentine adze blades increase in frequency, as do the antler wedges, and carefully shaped stone mauls begin to appear for the first time.

One of the most dramatic features surviving from Climax Period sites is the highly sophisticated and conventionalized art style that finds its expression in stone, bone, and antler carvings and in the incised petroglyphs and painted pictographs found in considerable numbers on the faces of the basalt cliffs, particularly along the rivers.

Although this art style apparently had its beginnings during the later phases of the previous period, it flourished during the Climax Period and reached its zenith just prior to the beginning of the Historic Period. Some of the carving is associated with utilitarian objects such as stone bowls, bone or antler combs, and stone pipes. Much of the carving appears also to be associated with ceremonial activities. Examples of this include the small bone and antler carvings of conventionalized human figures such as are found with cremation burials.

On islands in the Columbia River located at the important Priest Rapids fishery, deeply incised bedrock carvings of mythical creatures could be seen before that area was flooded by the Priest Rapids Dam. Nearly life-size human figurines, crudely carved in the round from large blocks of vesicular basalt, have been found at scattered localities along the Columbia River.

The source of this art style remains a puzzle. In some very general ways it resembles an art style of about the same time period that was in vogue in the Fraser River valley and neighboring regions of British Columbia. On the other hand, it resembles much more closely the elaborate art of the lower Columbia valley downstream from The Dalles, the territory of the Chinookan-speaking peoples. In light of present evidence, this art style appears to reflect an upstream movement of cultural influences. It may well go along with other lines of evidence indicating closer ties and trade relationships with down-stream peoples and with those along the coast.

Changes in housing can be seen in the Climax Period. During the early part of the period, housing was essentially as before: above ground and semisubterranean circular mat lodges. Although these styles persisted into the Climax Period, elongate mat lodges, both semisub-terranean and above ground, increased in fre-quency. These larger structures perhaps indicate that certain social changes were taking place, with a number of families now living together in a single structure. With increased mobility after the acquisition of the horse, the circular mat structure gave way in popularity to the circular skin-covered tipi. The elongate mat-covered house retained its popularity, however, as a winter dwelling. In late prehistoric times, a few rectangular plank houses began to appear in settlements in the vicinity of The Dalles, again evidence of upstream influence.

The Climax Period witnessed the full development of Yakima prehistoric culture that began in the area many thousands of years ago. It has been seen that throughout most of this time the prehistoric cultures matured slowly and in place, with little movement or evidence of significant outside contact. Yet late in the course of cultural development the pace of change began to increase as did the degree of contact with neighboring areas. Population increase, expanding trade relations, improved techniques for securing, processing, and storing food, elaborations in social and ceremonial life with an accompanying emphasis in the plastic and graphic arts, reached a peak by the beginning of the nineteenth Century. Then, suddenly, face-to-face contact with Euro-American culture occured.

The Historic Period began, technically, with the meeting of the Yakimas with members of the Lewis and Clark expedition in 1805. In fact, it is certain that metal tools and other kinds of nonnative materials were being introduced by trade in advance of this direct contact. At first,

PETROGLYPH AT THE DALES, "She Who Watches."

Photograph by Harvey S. Rice, Washington Archaeological Research Center

relations with early explorers and traders were peaceful and mutually advantageous. The basic way of life of the Yakima continued largely unaffected by this contact save for the substitution of metal for stone in such things as arrow points, axes, and knives. Many trade beads and bangles of glass and metal were introduced with a resultant increase in the ornamentation of clothing, ceremonial garb, and horse trappings.

Shortly, however, the introduction of diseases began to decimate the native population. The visitors' greed for land and their failure to even attempt to understand the needs, beliefs, and way of life of the Yakima, led to conflict and the ultimate reduction of Yakima territory to a fraction of its former size. In spite of the years of oppression, exploitation, and denial of basic human rights, the tough and resilient Yakima people have reemerged as a vigorous and prosperous nation. They have learned to take the good things from western culture – medical knowledge, education, and improved technology – while at the same time preserving the precious beliefs and traditions that provide the cohesiveness necessary for survival as a people.

LANGUAGE

The Treaty of 1855 brought together 14 tribes and bands, including speakers of three language families. Most of these groups, those occupying the central part of the territory, were speakers of languages of the Sahaptian family. The northernmost group, the Wenatchi and their subgroups — the Entiat, Chelan, and Methow — were speakers of languages belonging to the interior division of the Salishan family. And the Wishram, located near The Dalles on the Columbia River, spoke a language of the Chinookan family.

It is not possible from archaeological evidence to determine the length of time that these languages have been spoken in this area. It might be thought, however, that any archaeological evidence of sudden and dramatic change in cultural content might at least permit speculation about the possibility of an invading population, bringing with it a new language and a somewhat different technology. It has already been pointed out, however, that conservatism was the general rule in Yakima prehistory, and where change occurrred, it was never sudden and dramatic, even though late in their history the tempo of this change increased.

All that can be said at the moment, and this is based on linguistic rather than archaeological evidence, is that Sahaptian appears to have been spoken since earliest times in the area, and that there is some little evidence of an expansion of speakers of Salishan languages into the northern part of Yakima territory. Perhaps at a slightly earlier time an upriver expansion of Chinookanspeaking peoples took place. Whatever it means historically and culturally, it is interesting to note that the Yakima speakers of languages of the Sahaptian family occupy territory that is characterized by high temperatures, low rainfall, and sagebrush and bunchgrass vegetation. On the other hand, the Yakima Salishan and Chinookan speakers occur in areas that have a higher rainfall, more moderate temperature, and primarily a forest type vegetation.

Unfortunately, these languages are rapidly becoming extinct. The next few decades will no doubt see the last speakers disappear and with them an opportunity to learn more about these languages and their history.

TRADITIONAL WAY OF LIFE

Although 14 tribes and bands make up the modern Yakima Nation, the traditional cultures of all of these groups are in fact very similar to one another and, for a general understanding, may be treated as one. The differences that formerly existed among them were more often to be found in social and political life than in other areas of culture.

Fundamental to an understanding of Yakima political life is the recognition that, irrespective of the fact that some of the Yakima groups embraced tribal organization to a degree after contact with Plains Indians late in their history, the basic political unit of all groups was the village. It was in the village that the political

30

decisions were made that affected the daily lives of the Yakima. Where ideas of tribal organization began to make headway, these ideas related primarily to warfare and influenced everyday life scarcely at all. For most Yakima, the village was the largest political group.

It has often been noted that the political structure of many Indian groups of western North America has been poorly developed. Why is it then, among groups who have developed complex art styles, elaborate ceremonial activities, or advanced manufacturing technologies for example, that their political activities are so little structured? The answer appears to lie in the fact that because of their way of life the political problems are few and relatively uncomplicated, and in the fact that many of the political decisions, such as punishments for crimes, are made not by the entire village, but within the structure of the immediate family. Also, during the seasonal round of economic activities the winter village population would often break up into smaller units composed of one or more families. At these times the village ceased to exist as a political unit, and would only reemerge as such when the winter village was reoccupied in the late fall.

A related complicating factor is that the Yakima have always stressed the independence of the individual, and membership in a village community was quite fluid. Through inter-

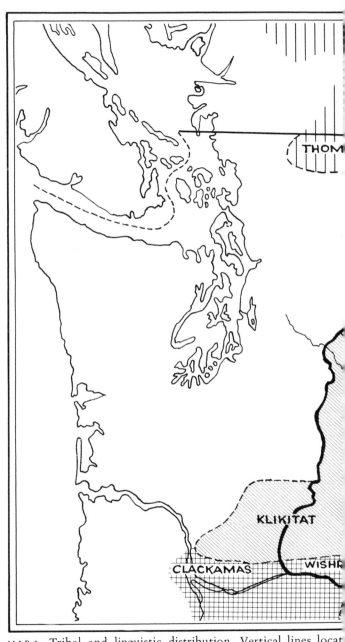

MAP 1. Tribal and linguistic distribution. Vertical lines locat
Salishan speakers; diagonal lines place Sahaptian speaker

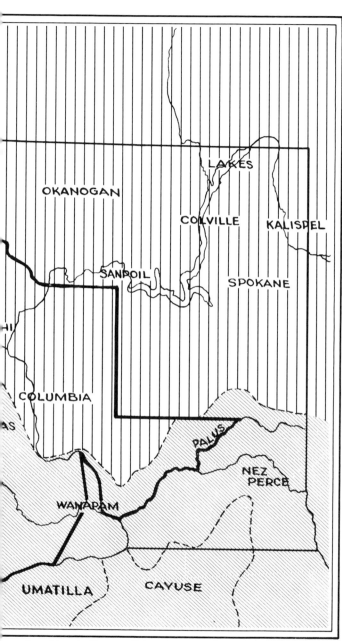

ross-hatching indicates Chinookan speakers. Dark line outlines riginal Yakima territory.

marriage with people in neighboring or distant villages, a wide network of relationships was established that made it possible for an individual or a family to be welcome for a few days, a few years, or permanently in some other village. This uncomplicated pattern of political affiliation should not be viewed simply as one at a rudimentary state of its development, but rather as one ideally adapted to hunting-fishing-gathering peoples for the maximum utilization of their environment without political restraints.

At first glance the idea of ownership of territory appears to have been rather poorly defined. Boundaries, particularly those away from the rivers, seem vague and unimportant. Nothing could be less true, for a number of very fundamental concepts lay behind Yakima ideas of territoriality. All peoples, whether agricultural or not, must entertain plans concerning the possible failure of a food resource. In the case of the Yakima, a poor fish run, a decline in the number of game animals, or a poor harvest of camas or huckleberries could have had serious economic consequences. As a result, in their concept of territoriality, a local group assumes stewardship over the economic resource of its area. Yet mutual utilization of the resources of a a number of these areas by members of different groups is not only possible but generally encouraged. This kind of territoriality is much more advantageous for all, because it not only reduces

34

economic risks, but makes possible expanded trade and social relationships.

With these ideas in mind it can be seen why particular resource-oriented localities assumed great importance. It is no accident that important villages, important trade centers, and important salmon fisheries coincided.

For large groups of people to come together for trade and social and ceremonial activities it was first of all necessary that the location could offer sufficient economic resources to support the group for the period of time involved. Obviously not all villages could be equally important in these matters, and thus it was that a number of centers developed which were surrounded by satellite communities. Such an area, for example, was at The Dalles or Long Narrows on the Columbia River. This was an important salmon fishery, a center of upstream and downstream trade as well as north-south trade, and the location of the principal Wishram village. Archaeological investigations indicate that the area for several miles around this locality shows evidence of many archaeological sites and that this settlement pattern has existed for thousands of years.

The informality in political structure is reflected in the patterns of leadership. Basically, a village leader was selected by the group on the basis of his abilities and because of his personal qualities and wisdom. He would be concerned with economic matters and with problems involving relationships with other villages. He would aid in settling disputes and would give advice if asked. His word was not absolute law and he was followed because of respect for him as a person and respect for his wisdom. Sometimes the leader of a large village would also act as the leader of neighboring smaller satellite communities of only a few houses.

With the coming of ideas about tribal organization came the idea of chiefs. These became important men and each was considered to be the chief of a number of villages. A chief functioned, however, primarily in those matters involving warfare and relationships with other bands or tribes. Each village continued to have a village leader for those matters involving its inhabitants' daily economic and social lives. A chief would usually function also as one of the local village leaders.

Late in the history of these peoples, the position of leadership tended to follow certain family lines. The position was not strictly hereditary for the person had to display the proper qualities before he would be followed, but unless certain persons were clearly not suited for the position, the tendency toward a loose hereditary leadership began to take place. The Wishram were an exception to the general situation that prevailed among the other Yakima. This group had a strong hereditary

36

leadership structure, and its leaders possessed a great deal of power. This no doubt is the result of strong influences from the coastal neighbors of the Wishram who followed a similar practice.

At the beginning of the Historic Period a number of types of housing or shelter were known and used depending upon the time of year, the location and the economic activities being pursued. Winter villages were composed of elongate A-frame type structures covered with several layers of matting fastened to the framework in shingle fashion. An opening was left at the top to allow the smoke to escape and the entrances were at the ends which were generally rounded in shape. Some circular mat lodges continued to be used and even skin covered tipis were sometimes used in winter. The latter were by far the most popular type of dwelling when the group or families moved about their territory as they followed their annual economic round, or when they travelled to visit other groups for purposes of trade or participation in social and ceremonial activities. Sometimes during the hot summer months a rectangular sunshade would be erected. Usually this structure had no walls and only a mat covered shed roof. These would be common at fishing sites along the rivers.

Another structure very important in the lives of the Yakima was the sweat house. This was used not only for the purpose of cleanliness, but had additional significance in matters pertaining to religious beliefs and the curing of illness. The Yakima considered the sweat bath to be a religious rite cleansing body and soul.

Sweat houses were of two basic types. The more substantial form was usually to be found near the principal villages and situated close to the river or a stream. These were semisubterranean structures with a pole framework and covered with mats and then with earth. Often these would be dug into the side of a river bank. A more temporary form of sweat house was built with a domelike framework of bent willow poles tied together and then covered with animal skins.

Sweat houses were used frequently by the Yakima and daily use by some men was not uncommon. To take a sweat bath it was first necessary to heat a number of rocks until they turned white. Usually vesicular basalt rocks were employed because these would heat uniformly due to their porosity and would not explode in the fire or in the sweat house. A small hole was dug in the floor of the sweat house just inside the door to accept the heated rocks and the entire floor of the interior would be covered with fresh grass or clean mats. Using tongs made from two pieces of wood some of the heated rocks would be moved from the fire to the pit inside the sweat house. A container of water was available and those taking the sweat bath would

RAMEWORK of temporary sweat lodge.

crawl into the sweat house and lower the flap at the door. The hot stones heated the interior of the sweat house, and water sprinkled on the hot rocks produced as much steam as was wanted. The duration of a sweat bath varied considerably, but at its conclusion the bathers would run down to the stream and plunge into the cool water. It is reported that in winter it was sometimes necessary to break the ice on the stream in order to be able to take the cold plunge following the sweat bath.

Fish drying racks and elevated platforms for storing mats and poles when a settlement was temporarily abandoned were other kinds of structures built by the Yakima. The Wishram built rectangular grave houses of planks and poles on islands in the Columbia.

We have seen that the economic round of the Yakima of the early Historic Period was the end product of thousands of years of development involving the improvement of equipment and techniques for utilizing the available food resources. By the time Lewis and Clark visited their territory along the Columbia River in 1805-1806, fishing was a major industry, and great quantities of dried salmon were being packed and shipped downstream for which the Yakima received desirable coastal products in return.

It appears that throughout Yakima territory fishing was the most productive economic activity. Gathering wild plant foods was probably second in importance and hunting was distant but important third.

The Columbia River and its tributaries contained a number of types of fish including five species of salmon *(Oncorhynchus)*, steelhead trout *(Salmo)*, sturgeon, sucker, trout, and lamprey. Of these, salmon were by far the most important as a source of food. Although there were salmon in the rivers at all times of the year, major runs attracted the Yakima to their fishing stations for weeks at a time. There was an early run of king salmon from January to March that was of but minor importance. The main run of kings occurred from late May until early July and these were accompanied by the oil-rich sockeye salmon. It was during this period that most of the year's supply of salmon was caught. From July until October or November silver salmon appear in considerable numbers. Steelhead trout are found in the rivers during most of the year, and many were caught during the fall, winter, and early spring. Midwinter was the period of the year when fishing for salmon was least productive, and a time when most economic activities reached their ebb.

Many techniques were used in the taking of salmon and steelhead trout, and each demanded a certain type of water condition and locality. One of the most productive techniques, and certainly the most dramatic, was that of dip-

DIPNETTING SALMON on the Klickitat River.

Photograph by Harvey S. Rice, Washington Archaeological Research Center

netting for fish. The best place to dipnet salmon was where the waters were forced through narrow channels and over low falls, crashing and tumbling from one turbulent pool to another. From wooden platforms precariously tied to the basalt cliffs and hanging over the whirlpools and eddies, the fisherman swept his long-handled dipnet from the upper to the lower end of the pool. In some places the fish could be seen, but mostly the water was so turbulent that the fish could only be felt as it swam into the net. Such fishing stations were highly prized and were inherited from generation to generation. Permission to fish at a station could be obtained from the owner.

In the fall when the water was low and clear fish could be speared with two-pronged toggling harpoons. This device is identical to those used on the coast for salmon, and looks like a smaller version of the coastal sealing harpoon. The harpoon consisted of a long pointed pole with another shorter, divergent prong fastened at an angle to the first approximately 20 inches from the distal end. To each was fastened a toggling harpoon head consisting of two barbs made of elk or deer bone with a central bone point. Both harpoon points were detachable from the shaft and had a line attached to them that was held by the fisherman. Sometimes light colored rocks would be placed on the stream bottom so that the fish could be more clearly seen.

The leister appears to be a rather recent addition to the fishing gear of the Yakima. This device consisted of a long pole with two short, diverging prongs on the end which were about eight to ten inches long. At the tip of these prongs bone points were attached so that they angled backward toward the handle and each other. When this spear was forced over the back of a salmon the prongs sprang outward and the backward pointing barbs penetrated the side of the fish and held it securely. The leister has not been reported for coastal tribes, but is well known among Eskimo groups in the far north. How it came into the hands of the Yakima is a mystery.

Fish weirs and traps also were productive means of taking fish. Both were used more commonly on the smaller rivers and streams than on the Columbia and Snake rivers. A fish weir was simply a blockade placed temporarily across the stream. It was constructed of poles and wattle-work in such a way that the water could pass through but the migrating salmon or steelhead were blocked from moving upstream. Fish trying to get past this obstruction could be readily caught with dipnets.

The traps were of several types, but a common design is one that was used just below a low fall in the stream. This device worked on the principal that fish will often permit themselves to be carried backwards downstream for short distances and were, therefore, washed into these basketlike traps from which they could not escape.

In historic times the Yakima have effectively employed the gill net for catching salmon, and they insist that they also used this type of net in prehistoric times. They report that huge gill nets, nearly twenty feet deep and as long as needed, were made from a split root called Ta-cush. These nets were buried in the sand between fishing seasons to preserve them.

Although some of the fish caught was eaten fresh, most of it was dried and preserved for future use. At the height of the salmon runs the catching, butchering, and drying of the fish employed most of the people in the village.

After the fish was thoroughly dried much of it, particularly the chinook salmon and the male steelhead, was pulverized by pounding it in a mortar with a long pestle. This pulverized meat was then carefully packed in baskets and stored for winter use. In this form it would keep for a long time in the arid climate of the inter-montane region.

The technique of preparing this highly con-centrated protein food, a few ounces of which could serve as a full meal, is undoubtedly of great antiquity, and may well have made poss-ible a relatively secure economic life throughout most of their history.

A wide variety of mammals was hunted for

food, skins, and for bone, horn, and antler — the raw materials used in manufacturing tools and weapons. Deer were hunted throughout the year by individuals or by organized groups carrying out carefully planned drives. Sometimes dogs were used in these game drives. The principal weapon was the bow and arrow. In the summer and early fall many families went into the mountains expressly to hunt elk and gather huckleberries and roots. The meat of deer and elk was often eaten fresh, but at the mountain hunting camps the intention was to secure as much meat as possible and dry it for use during the winter months. The hides were fleshed, scraped, and tanned and would soon be converted into skin garments and moccasins. Rawhide was used in the manufacture of folded hide containers, identical except for the decorative design to the parfleche of the Plains Indians. Leather thongs that had been soaked and stretched were used for tying countless things and for lacing snowshoes used during the winter hunts.

Bears were hunted primarily for their fur and for the claws and teeth which could be used as ornaments or incorporated as decorative elements in the elaborate and impressive ceremonial garb. Bears, wolves, foxes, and cougars, animals that could be attracted to bait, were usually caught in deadfalls made of logs and heavy rocks.

In former times the mountain sheep were abundant in Yakima territory and could be found in the hills or along rocky cliffs bordering stretches of the Columbia river. By the time the Lewis and Clark expedition reached the area, however, mountain sheep seem to have entirely disappeared. In addition to providing meat and skins, the horns of these animals were used for making spoons and ladles which often had elaborate designs carved into their surface. Mountain goats were occasionally hunted among the high mountain peaks and the horns of these animals also could be cut and shaped into attractive functional utensils.

Along the rivers and in marshy areas waterfowl were hunted with bows and arrows in the spring and fall. The eggs of ducks and geese that had wintered locally could be gathered in the spring.

Eagles were hunted not for food but for the feathers that were needed for ceremonial regalia.

The gathering of a large variety of vegetal products, whether food plants or the raw materials for weaving mats and baskets, was primarily the task of women. Of the numbers of food plants sought, some formed the staple items in the diet while others were distinctly food supplements. Camas was the staple of the entire region, and after the women had dug huge quantities of these roots with their short, curved digging sticks, the roots would be pit roasted and prepared for storage. Wild onions, wild carrots, and wild potatoes also were eagerly sought. One type of wild potato known as "Wapatoo" was another vegetable staple and very important to the Yakima. There were other types of plants that were gathered for their leaves and stems. In some parts of Yakima territory acorns and hazelnuts could be found. In contrast to the food patterns of the Indians of California, these items did not figure prominently in the diet of the Yakima peoples. Nor did they do much seed gathering as did the peoples of the Great Basin area to the south.

Berries, particularly huckleberries, were gathered in large quantities and prepared for winter use.

A type of black, hairlike moss found growing in the mountains was collected, soaked, washed, roasted, and then formed into cakes for storage. The Yakima have long had a sizeable list of medicines prepared from vegetable products. They even collected certain types of roots with which to flavor their two types of tobacco.

The basic techniques of cooking food involved pit roasting, roasting over an open fire, and boiling by means of heated stones dropped into stone, wooden, or water-tight basket containers of liquid. Usually two meals, a morning meal and an evening meal, were prepared each day. The food was served in wooden bowls or horn containers and probably even the watertight baskets were used for this purpose.

The economic life of the Yakima can be characterized as one of many cooperative activities. The harvesting of salmon during the annual runs was a busy, active time involving numbers of people fishing, tending traps and weirs, and butchering and drying the fish. Hunting often involved game drives by many men, and the digging of roots and the picking of berries was accomplished by women's work parties.

Trade likewise involved cooperative relationships between a man and his trading partners from other groups. These carefully nurtured, enduring relationships were characterized by mutual fairness and trust, and made possible the acquisition of many items and materials not locally available. Primarily, Yakima trade involved exchanging products of the interior for products of the coast. At the major trading center at The Dalles, skins, fur, oil, shells, roots, pemmican, feathers, robes, clothing, baskets, canoes, horses, and slaves were exchanged. When the white fur traders arrived at The Dalles early in the Historic Period, they were not particularly welcome because the Wishram and other local traders resented the direct trade between the fur trader and other tribes which resulted in the loss of their position as middlemen in the transactions.

50

The Yakima were a highly mobile people, particularly after they acquired the horse from northern Great Basin tribes around the middle of the eighteenth century. Some have placed the date as early as 1730 AD. The horses multiplied rapidly and soon large herds roamed over the land. Not only were horses a means of transportation but they also rapidly became an item of wealth and status.

The Yakima also had canoes which they used principally along the major rivers. Some of the tribes and bands whose principal villages were along the Columbia could be described as basically river people. Much of their lives was spent on the river catching the various kinds of fish available to them. Although canoes were an essential item in their fishing activities, they seldom made long canoe voyages, preferring horses to canoes for long trips.

The canoes were primarily of the shovel-nose type hollowed out from a single log. They made them in a variety of sizes from ten feet to over 20 feet in length. Occasionally a coastal style of canoe with a raised bow and stern was traded upstream. Canoes were paddled in deep water but were usually poled along the shallows.

The dress of the Yakima varied considerably depending upon the time of year and the type of activity in which they were engaged. Generally, the summer time garb of the men was a breech-clout, a skin vest, and a fur robe if

THE LAST SURVIVING shovel-nose canoe at fishing camp.

Relander Collection, Yakima Regional Library

needed. Moccasins were available but were worn mostly in the winter. This garb would be augmented by leggings, trousers, and a fur hat in cold weather.

Conventional summer dress for a woman was a short woven skirt or an apron-like affair hanging down front and back. Upper garments, if worn, were not unlike those of the men. Later in their history buckskin dresses and leggings similar to Plains Indian styles became the universal style of clothing. Often these garments were attractively ornamented with porcupine quill embroidery and later with glass trade beads. Women frequently wore a basket hat that had the shape of a truncated cone. These hats were approximately ten inches high and four inches across at the top. They were finely woven and ornamented with designs woven into them by means of an overlay technique using colored grass.

With the gradual adoption of Plains patterns of warfare and recording war honors, the Yakima men also adopted the feather headdress as part of their own ceremonial regalia. Patterns of decoration, however, carried the distinct stamp of the Yakima.

Prior to the introduction of metal tools and containers the Yakima had made a close and comfortable adjustment to their environment and to the raw materials this environment had to offer, including those things that could be

54

KIMA IN CEREMONIAL REGALIA.

obtained through native trade networks. Arrow heads, spearpoints, knives, drills, spokeshaves, and scrapers were flaked from fine cryptocrystalline materials such as chalcedony and opal that occurred locally as impurities in the basalt flows. Gingko petrified forest with its great tree trunks of opalized fossil wood is located within Yakima territory. The abundance of this raw material helped to produce some of North America's most skilled artisans in the techniques of pressure flaking and percussion flaking of stone tools. Some of their stone implements and containers such as pestles and mortars, were shaped by a pecking and grinding technique. A variety of tools and handles for tools were manufactured from bone and antler. Needles, awls and parts of composite fishing devices such as harpoons, leisters, and gaffs were shaped by cutting, grinding, and polishing there materials. Bows, arrows, and the shafts of spears and harpoons, as well as a number of other tools and weapons were made from wood. Teeth and shell were used primarily for ornamentation.

The art of making woven baskets, bags, and mats was highly developed among the Yakima women. Mats from three to six feet wide and sometimes more than 20 feet long were made by sewing together the stems of tule or cattail. Some mats were made from grass by a special twining technique. Mats were used as coverings for houses, as rugs for the floor, and as mattresses for the beds.

No doubt the most numerous items to be found in a household were the baskets and soft twined bags that were used for gathering, cooking, and storing food, and also for storing a wide variety of personal possessions. The use of pottery and the techniques for making it were never developed in this area, probably because the relatively heavy and easily broken pots were not suited to their seminomadic way of life. All of the basic weaving techniques – twining, coiling, and plaiting – were known and skillfully employed by the Yakima women to produce baskets, soft bags, and wallets. It is reported that some of the groups made rabbit skin blankets. By cutting a dried rabbit skin in a spiral fashion, long strips were produced that served as the blanket warp elements. The weft was made from a type of grass that was rolled into a cord on the thigh. Some groups probably used mountain sheep and mountain goat wool for making blankets, but there is no firm record of this. Packstraps and tumplines were either woven or made from animal skins.

PERSONAL DEVELOPMENT

As was generally characteristic of Plateau peoples, the Yakima had a high regard for the rights and privileges of the individual, and from infancy a person would be trained to be self-sufficient yet at the same time respectful of others. Shortly after a child was born it was placed in a cradleboard on a soft pad where it was covered with a decorated buckskin and securely tied in. Here the child would spend much of its time until it was weaned. This convenient way of carrying the child enabled a woman to carry on her customary economic and household activities knowing that the infant was comfortable and secure.

Throughout their childhood the youngsters learned the skills and techniques that would be essential in their adult life, for many of their games were play imitations of adult activities. Boys played with small bows and arrows, and girls were provided with the necessary materials so that they too could play at making baskets and clothing. The myths and stories and the traditional lore of the tribe were imparted to the youngsters by aged relatives. Much of the training of a child was informal and by precept. At times, however, rigorous activities were prescribed. Boys were admonished to be strong and they would be trained to hunt and travel with great endurance.

Although there was some variation among the Yakima groups, particularly in the way the ceremonies were conducted, among all, the receiving of a name was one of the most

58

important occasions in a person's life. An individual would receive several names during his lifetime, an informal one as an infant, but later, names that were of great importance and held in high regard. Usually the naming ceremony was accompanies by the giving of gifts by the parents of the child to those in attendance at the ceremony.

When a child reached puberty it really marked a significant change in his status for at this time the individual left the play and informal activities of children and entered the company of adults. With the boys there was little formal recognition of this fact, but girls were isolated briefly and given training by an older female relative concerning the duties of a woman and a wife. At the end of the period of isolation a ceremony of notification was held which involved dancing and the distribution of small gifts.

The Yakima strictly regulated the relationships between unmarried young men and young women. Marriage was a formally arranged affair and accompanied by an exchange of gifts between the families involved. It was not uncommon for a man or woman to marry outside of his or her local village community, and through this mechanism a broad network of kin relationships was established. The cross utilization of economic resources among various groups was facilitated by these marriage patterns. A married couple usually, but not always, resided in the groom's parents' village.

Unlike some Plateau groups, the Yakima had developed ideas about wealth and status differences among individuals. Through proper spiritual guidance, through hard work, through skillful trading activities, and through demonstrated ability as a warrior, the way was open for a man to achieve a position of respect and influence in his local group. For particularly successful individuals this reputation might spread far beyond his village. Slavery was known to the Yakima but it was primarily among the Wishram that this institution had much significance. As the principal traders along the Columbia River the Wishram traded slaves to coastal groups where the possession of slaves was of great social importance. The Wishram held slaves as items to barter and, to a degree, to elevate their own status in imitation of the practice along the Northwest Coast. Slavery, as an institution, did not fit well with the beliefs in the rights and dignity of the individual held so strongly by the Yakima.

Throughout their childhood the young people in a Yakima village were informally schooled in the religious beliefs of their people. They attended the winter spirit dances, they witnessed the spirit power of successful individuals, and they stood by in awe and silence as the shaman used his power to cure the sick. Then as these children reached the age of about ten, the informality was exchanged for formal tutoring by an older relative. A young boy, and often young girls as well, would embark on a series of one-night quests to attempt to secure a spirit power. The seeker of this power visited sacred places and attempted to stay awake and alert so that when the spirit came and identified itself the visionary would recognize it and would learn the song that came with the spiritual help and guidance. These were intensely personal experiences and would not be revealed to anyone.

It was believed that success in life was based upon the spiritual assistance given to an individual, and without such help no one could hope to succeed.

The principal religious practitioner was the shaman who carried on his curing and other religious activities on a part-time basis. He was paid for his services, but he still had to participate in the economic life of the community. The shaman's powers were usually considered greater than those of others, but not necessarily of a different kind.

After a period of contact with the white traders, trappers, missionaries, and settlers, the religious beliefs of the Yakima began to change. It was a selective change, however, embracing those aspects of Christianity that attracted them, rejecting others, and preserving much of the old.

EARLY EURO-AMERICAN CONTACT

The voyages of exploration along the Northwest Coast of America in the late 1700's by the Spaniards, Britons, Russians, and Americans, showered gift and trade items on the local coastal groups. By way of the trading center at The Dalles, these items soon began to appear among the Yakima. When Lewis and Clark reached the Wishram villages in 1805 on their historic expedition across the western part of the continent, they reported that the people there already were in the possession of metal tools. It is clear that some trade items of Euro-American culture were reaching the Yakima prior to face-to-face contact.

Unknown to the Yakima a number of developments had already taken place far from their homeland that were to have a profound impact on their future way of life.

The initial period of exploration along the coastal waters of Washington was quickly followed by a brisk trade in sea otter skins. In May of 1792 Captain Robert Gray sailed across the bar of the Columbia River and spent nine days exploring and trading for furs. Gray was soon followed by many other American traders with dreams of huge profits to be made in the maritime fur trade. The system was to purchase cheap trade goods in the ports along the east coast of the United States, sail around South America and up to the Northwest coast where these items were traded for sea otter skins. The furs would then be taken to Chinese ports where they were sold at great profit and where Asian goods could be purchased and carried around South Africa, back to the east coast ports of the United States where yet another profit could be made. Although this trading pattern lasted but a short time until the coastal tribes became economically more sophisticated and began demanding more goods for their furs, and the Asian markets become glutted with sea otter skins, the maritime fur trade introduced the world to the Northwest Coast, and indirectly to the interior lands that lay beyond the coastal strip.

The interior lands, however, were really opened up by the overland fur trade in beaver and other fur-bearing animal skins. As early as the mid-1600's the British were developing a fur trade system in northeast Canada, and in 1670 the Hudson Bay Company was established, securing a monopoly on trade in the region drained by Hudson Bay. Competition came from French fur traders who explored westward, gradually extending their territory beyond the Great Lakes, and from independent British traders. To compete successfully against the Hudson Bay Company, many of the independent traders merged to form the Northwest Company. They employed as many of the French-Canadian traders and trappers as they could, and the colorful "voyageurs" continued pushing westward as the trapping areas of the east became exhausted. In July of 1793 a British trader, Alexander Mackenzie and his companions, paddled down the Bella Coola River in what is now British Columbia and reached the Pacific Ocean after crossing the continent by land. Mackenzie was followed by other traders and explorers. After a trip down the river which was later named for him, Simon Fraser reached the coast in 1808. Another Northwest Company employee, David Thompson, established a trading post on the Upper Columbia River near Lake Windermere in 1807. In 1808, he continued his trading and explorations and in 1809 established a trading post on the present Lake Pend Oreille in northern Idaho and another post in northern Montana.

By 1810, the Northwest Company had established a trading post at the mouth of the Spokane River. This post, called Spokane House, was to become one of the main trading centers in the Pacific Northwest.

On July 15, 1811, David Thompson reached the mouth of the Columbia River after a downstream canoe journey from Spokane House. He discovered that representatives of an American fur company, the Astor Company, had already established themselves there, having come from the east by ship.

The successes of the British enterpreneurs in

the western fur trade stimulated the American government to begin explorations for an overland route to the Pacific with the ultimate aim of breaking what amounted to a virtual monopoly by the British traders of the lucrative fur industry. The Lewis and Clark expedition was the initial step toward this goal.

The noose of western culture was beginning to tighten around the Yakima. Influences were now beginning to impinge upon them from all directions. When John Jacob Astor established the Astor Company he envisioned a series of trading posts scattered through the vast country from the Rockies to the Pacific. From these posts furs would flow down the drainages leading to the Columbia River, thence down the Columbia itself to the main post at the mouth of the river, and then by ship to the eastern market. This would avoid the time consuming and costly shipping of furs eastward by overland routes.

In quick succession trading posts were established at a number of points, but the War of 1812 panicked the Astorians and they hastily sold their posts to the Northwest Company for fear they would be seized by the British.

Competition between the Northwest Company and the Hudson Bay Company ended in 1821 when the two companies merged, retaining the name of the latter. The company decided to strengthen its holdings in the west and John

McLoughlin was chosen to build a substantial trading post on the lower Columbia. During the period from 1824-1834, Fort Vancouver was constructed, grew, and flourished. The large stockade contained over 30 buildings including carpenter shops, blacksmith shops, a store, a schoolhouse, and a chapel. The impact of this trading center was felt throughout the Columbia drainage and the Yakima rapidly acquired many trade items including axes, knives, and guns.

The way of life of the Yakima was now beginning to change even more. Although remaining independent of much face-to-face contact with western culture, they were becoming dependent more than they were aware on the metal tools and weapons of the traders. With these new additions to their culture old tasks were made easier and food became more abundant. The leisure time produced by the surpluses in food was spent travelling and trading. Increased ties were forged with the tribes of the Plains east of the Rockies. Warring raids with their traditional enemies, the Shoshonean-speaking peoples in central Oregon, increased in frequency. And their increasing wealth and mobility brought together larger and larger groups of people for trading, horse racing, and social activities.

The Hudson Bay Company began to have competition from American traders in the late 1820's, and during the 1830's the numbers of independent trading expeditions continued to increase and new kinds of influences began to be felt by the Yakima. Missionaries began arriving and establishing themselves among neighboring groups. The Yakima had long observed some of the religious practices of the traders and explorers, but now the first attempts were being made in the Northwest to educate and Christianize the Indians. Although no missions were yet established in Yakima territory, the Yakima were mobile people and through their contacts with others began to learn something of the Christian religion. Jason Lee's Methodist Mission in the Willamette valley of Oregon founded in the 1830's became the center of a population growth by white settlers.

The next group of missionaries to reach the Northwest were the Whitmans and the Spauldings. The Whitmans established their mission at Waiilatpu near the present city of Walla Walla, Washington. The Spauldings settled in Nez Perce territory, establishing their mission near the town now known as Lapwai. Both missions were distant enough to make visits by Yakima infrequent. The indirect impact on the Yakima was, however, very significant and far reaching. For one thing, the Protestant missionaries actively encouraged more and more settlers to come to the northwest which soon led to a greatly increased immigrant traffic over the Oregon Trail. The white settlers moving into the area brought with them diseases such as smallpox and measles to which the native populations had no immunity. In time epidemics of disastrous proportions were to ravage all of the native groups.

The Mission groups, assisted by the settlers who followed, introduced agriculture to the Indian peoples, and it is surprising how rapidly farming and stock raising spread throughout the Plateau tribes, altering their traditional economic patterns and making them dependent upon a new way of life.

Tragically, the Whitmans are best remembered by the massacre of fourteen of their group by Cayuse Indians who suspected them of being responsible for the deaths of many Cayuse people by causing an epidemic of measles. The massacre prompted the Oregon Provisional Government to organize a small volunteer army of 537 men for the purpose of pursuing and punishing the Cayuse. This became the so-called Cayuse War of 1848-50, and marked the first official confrontation between a Plateau tribe and the white settlers. Unfortunately, it was not to be the last.

Encouragement by the missionaries, a severe economic depression in the east, the tales of a bountiful land with a good climate and, for some, the search for adventure in the new lands, all contributed to the increasing flow of settlers between 1840 and 1860. The rapidly growing immigrant population west of the Cascades began to make demands for law and government. The families of farmers, trappers, and traders were soon clamoring for schools and for a militia to protect them from Indian attacks. They needed courts and judges to regulate marriage, to settle conflicting claims to land, and to settle the estates of those who died. In rapid succession a provisional government for Oregon was established in 1843, the first taxes were levied in 1844, and the first governor was elected in 1845. The northern boundary of this political unit was to be the same as that of the United States. In 1846 the disputed claims of Great Britain and the United States as to which government actually owned most of this land were amicably settled by deciding that the boundary should be at the forty-ninth parallel, thereby giving the territory of what are now the states of Oregon and Washington to the United States. When this decision was made the Hudson Bay Company moved its western headquarters from Fort Vancouver on the Lower Columbia River to Vancouver Island.

Oregon Territory was finally established by an Act of Congress in 1848, but this had scarcely been done when the settlers living north of the Columbia River, particularly those living around Puget Sound, began objecting to having to travel all the way to the Willamette Valley in order to carry on their legal business, and began pressing for a division that would make the area north of the Columbia River a separate political entity. In 1853, the President signed a bill which created the Washington Territory.

A few years earlier, in 1850, at the urging of settlers, Congress passed the Donation Land Act which was to apply to lands lying west of the Cascade Mountains. The purpose of this act was to provide land for the settlers, 320 acres for a single person and 640 acres for a married couple. Obviously this land that was being claimed by the settlers belonged to one or another Indian group, and the act, therefore, also provided for relocation of the Indian peoples. The native peoples were scarcely consulted, and there was even a rumor that all Indian groups living west of the Cascades were to be moved to the interior. The rumor had a very unsettling effect on the interior groups.

For the most part, however, these activities and political developments were scarcely known and largely ignored by the Yakima. Most of the contacts between the white settlers and the Indian groups were taking place west of the Cascades at this time. A few settlers had begun to move into Yakima territory, and although they were not particularly welcomed, they were accommodated without threats or violence.

At the time Washington became a Territory the President appointed Major Isaac F. Stevens to be the Governor and also to hold the position of Superintendent of Indian Affairs. Stevens,

70

who had graduated at the head of his West Point class and who had served with distinction in the Mexican War, had experience as a surveyor and was noted for his vigorous and decisive action.

On the way to his new position he led a survey party in search of a feasible railroad route to the Pacific Northwest. Stevens directed another survey party headed by George McClellan to proceed to the Northwest by ship and to begin explorations for the route from the west, across the Cascades, and to attempt to meet the Stevens party en route from the east. Neither group had much success in finding a route through the Cascades that year. Later Stevens again sent McClellan to reconnoiter the Cascade passes and to attempt to find a more direct wagon trail from Walla Walla to Puget Sound. In the fall of 1853 the first group of settlers passed through Yakima territory and over Naches Pass on their way to Fort Steilacoom on Puget Sound. Thus began the unofficial opening up of Yakima lands to travelers, settlers, and miners.

As Superintendent of Indian Affairs as well as Governor of the Territory, Stevens felt that it was his duty to conclude treaties with the Indians as soon as possible, in part to head off impending conflicts and in part to open more land to white settlement. In 1854 Stevens organized a Treaty Commission and by 1855 he had concluded treaties with the principal groups west of the Cascades. Pleased with these early successes he was eager to conclude similar agreements with those tribes and bands lying east of the mountains.

In anticipation of his treaty negotiations Stevens had, in 1854, appointed Mr. A. J. Bolon to be the Indian Agent for the Territory. Stevens also sent the secretary of the Treaty Commission, James Doty, to the interior to meet with the leaders of the various tribes and bands. He was to prepare them for a general meeting to be held in the late spring or early summer of 1855 at which time treaties were to be signed. Throughout these preliminary negotiations the Yakima chiefs were reluctant even to discuss such a meeting but finally were prevailed upon to attend.

Governor Stevens had little understanding of the differences between the west coast tribes and those of the interior, particularly as to how they viewed their ownership of their land. Except in a few instances, the coastal tribes has never really been threatened by settlers taking up the wooded lands surrounding their villages and salmon streams. Not fully understanding the potential impact of the treaty negotiations they believed that as long as they retained title to their streams and villages they would be little affected by the treaties.

The different form of economic life led by interior tribes and bands made them view their lands in a much different way. All of their territory was of importance to them for the different types of resources that occurred in different areas. Opening part of this land to settlement meant that those portions would be forever inaccessible. Their ties to the land were in part religious and strongly emotional. Stevens was to discover that it was going to be much more difficult to get the interior groups to sign the treaties, to understand their full implications and, lacking the understanding, to adhere to their provisions.

On a Tuesday afternoon, May 28, 1855, the Treaty Council was convened at Walla Walla. The Yakima were represented by five of their chiefs, Kamiakin, Owhi, Skloom, Teias, and Shawawai.

Kamiakin, their principal chief, has been described as a natural leader with an imposing appearance and was also a man of considerable wealth. He was the son of a Yakima woman from an important family and a Palouse man who had the reputation of being a skilled warrior. He was the first Yakima to begin raising cattle, having exchanged some of his horses at Fort Vancouver for a small herd. In 1847 he had invited Catholic missionaries to come and instruct his people. Kamiakin's home was located near the Ahtanum Mission although he reportedly spent much of his time in Medicine Valley.

Owhi, Kamiakin's half-brother, was the

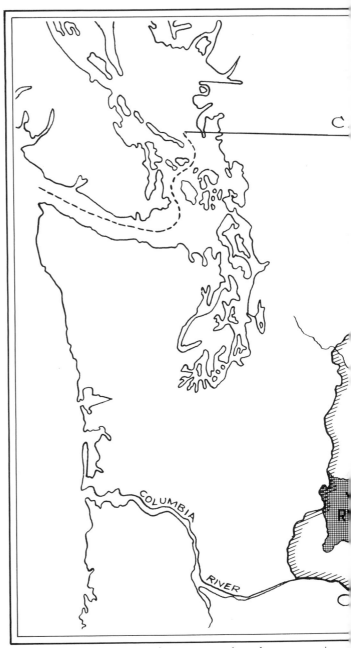

MAP 2. Yakima territory before treaty and modern reservation.

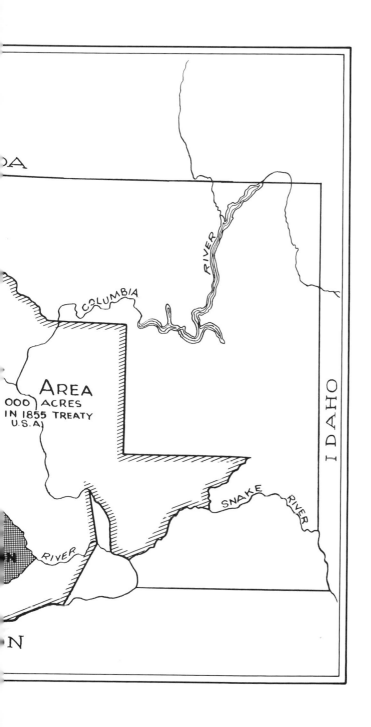

leader of those Yakima whose territory was from the Naches River north. He is said to have been tall and impressive in appearance.

Skloom was Kamiakin's brother and lived in the vicinity of where Fort Simcoe now stands.

Teias was the father of Kamiakin's wife. The final member of the group was Shawawai.

An estimated 5,000 Indians representing many tribes and bands camped at the Council grounds. Nearly 2,500 Nez Perce, led by Lawyer, one of their principal chiefs, reached the encampment on May 24. The Yakima delegation had few of their people with them for this was the time for catching salmon and digging roots. Palouse, Walla Walla, Cayuse, Umatilla and other smaller groups were represented.

The treaty Council lasted for two weeks during which time the main points of the treaty were explained to the Indian leaders. The Nez Perce appeared most eager to sign but the Yakima generally were opposed to the whole idea. There were to be three reservations, one for the Nez Perce, one for the Walla Walla, Cayuse, and Umatilla, and one for the Yakima.

As the Council dragged on day after day, Governor Stevens was becoming impatient with the Yakima chiefs who refused to sign and wished to have another meeting at a later time. Finally, after considerable pressure was applied by Stevens, the Yakima chiefs, who by now wished to go back to their people, signed the treaty on the 9th of June.

Under the terms of the treaty the Yakima agreed to cede 16,920 square miles of their territory, retaining only 1,875 square miles for their exclusive use. The Yakima were to be reimbursed for improvements they had made upon the lands to be ceded. Article III provided that roads could be run through the reservation for public convenience. The exclusive right of taking fish in all streams running through and bordering the reservation, and at all "usual and accustomed places," as well as the right to hunting, gethering roots and berries, and to pasturing their horses and cattle on open and unclaimed lands were guaranteed to the Yakima by the treaty.

The treaty stated that the United States was to establish two schools, one of which was to be an agricultural and industrial school. Further, they were to build two blacksmith's shops, a tin shop, a gunsmith's shop, a carpenter's shop, and a wagon and ploughmaker's shop. In addition, the confederated tribes and bands of the Yakima were to receive a payment of $140,000 over a twenty year period.

The treaty designated Kamiakin as the head chief of the tribe, a position that was soon to become war chief.

Article XI of the treaty stated that the treaty would become obligatory upon the contracting parties as soon as it was ratified by the President and the Senate of the United States. The treaty was not ratified immediately, and information was erroneously published in the territorial newspaper that the Yakima lands were open for settlement. Believing that the government was not living up to its part of the bargain to keep settlers and travelers off the reservation, the Yakima decided to kill all white trespassers. A party of miners passing through Yakima country was killed by a group of Indians. Agent Bolon, hearing of the deaths, decided to investigate and was killed by a group of Yakima whom he met on the trail. Bolon's death brought soldiers and the beginning of the war.

Two companies of troops were sent into Yakima country. Major Granville Haller with 84 men was dispatched from The Dalles. Lieutenant W. A. Slaughter led 50 men through Naches Pass.

Kamiakin and his warriors met Major Haller's company near Toppenish Creek and after a series of skirmishes over a period of several days sent them retreating back to The Dalles. Hearing of Haller's defeat, Slaughter and his troops fled back through Naches Pass.

Major Gabriel Rains, commander of the federal troops at Vancouver then took soldiers into the Yakima country and he, too, was forced to retreat to The Dalles.

General John Wool, commander of all of the

U.S. soldiers on the Pacific Coast, closed the eastern part of Washington Territory to further settlement.

A series of minor conflicts occurred as the war dragged on. It was generally felt by the military authorities that an all-out war with the Indians would not be necessary. This belief was changed in May of 1858 when Colonel Steptoe with 158 men on an investigation mission to the Spokane and Colville tribes, was decisively beaten and forced to retreat at the battle of Rosalia, near what is now called Steptoe Butte.

On August 6, 1858, Colonel George Wright with a command of 700 men left Fort Walla Walla for Spokane country. After one abortive attack the Spokane came to surrender. Colonel Wright's men rounded up over 800 horses and killed them, believing that this would leave the Indians helpless. He was apparently correct in his assumption for a number of other groups soon surrendered. Several Indian leaders were killed including Owhi of the Yakima. Kamiakin did not surrender but went to his family land at Rock Lake southwest of Spokane. He refused to return to the Yakima Reservation fearing the whites and believing he would be held accountable for any misdeeds. He died in peace and in poverty in 1877 at the age of 73.

When Kamiakin refused to return to the reservation, Spencer of the Klickitats was appointed chief and served briefly. Joe Stwire or

CEREMONIAL HOUSE and flag of religious cult at Priest Rapids.

Relander Collection, Yakima Regional Library

White Swan was then elected chief and served until he died. His brother Reverend Stwire G. Waters who was a Methodist minister was elected to succeed him. He served as chief until he died in 1932.

After the treaty was ratified in 1859, the Yakima Agency headquarters was moved from its original location at White Salmon to Fort Simcoe which had been turned over to the Indian Department by the army, A succession of agents and superintendents served the Yakima, but one of the better known and more successful was the Reverend James A. Wilbur, a Methodist missionary. Rev. Wilbur came to the Yakima in 1860 and was appointed agent in 1864. He served in that position until 1882.

The early days of the new reservation were chaotic. Following the war the Yakima people were scattered, dispirited, and in poverty. The war and the giving up of much of their land under the articles of the treaty had disrupted the old seasonal economic round. A major effort was made to plant crops and orchards, to fence land, and to secure great amounts of salmon during the seasonal runs. Gradually things began to improve as they became more self-sufficient. A series of less than competent agents and subagents undoubtedly slowed their economic progress.

In 1866 a stage road was opened over Satus pass, and by 1875, 3,500 head of cattle carried the Indian brand and their horses numbered over 16,000.

The Northern Pacific Railroad was completed through the Yakima Reservation in 1885, bringing a slight increase in prosperity to the Indians.

The Yakima appear always to have been a deeply religious people. Their traditional belief in spitual guidance to make them successful or to help them through difficult times permits us to understand the religious responses that were made after they were placed on the reservation, lacking in food, shelter, and leadership.

Throughout the western United States, in the period of social upheaval and disorganization that traditionally followed contact with Euro-American culture, a number of messianic religious movements sprang up and spread rapidly from tribe to tribe. These religious cults were based upon the native religion plus added elements from Christianity. They involved the pattern of a leader or messiah who was said to have died and after a visit to the land of the dead, returned to life to spread a message to his people. This message usually contained statements telling the people to love one another and to live in peace. As a consequence of leading this good life, those who had died would be reborn. The animals and fish would return, and the earth would be renewed. Explicit in many of these messages was the statement that the whites would disappear, never to return. The ritual associated with these religious observances often involved dancing and drumming, and the ceremonial eating of food and drinking of water. The Ghost Dance Religion of the Great Basin that spread so rapidly among Plains Indian tribes is such a messianic cult.

The genesis of these religious movements will never be fully known, but studies have indicated that the ancestral form from which all of these movements developed, including the Ghost Dance, began among the Plateau Indians at least as early as the late 1700's. This ancestral form has been called the Prophet Dance to distinguish it from later, historically known and named religious movements.

In the beginning the Prophet Dance was based entirely upon native religous beliefs. Elements of Christianity, mainly Catholicism, were introduced by eastern Indian groups even before direct face-to-face contacts with explorers, missionaries, and settlers had taken place. In the 1830's, particularly, many additional Christian elements were included in the Prophet Dance Religion.

The Smohalla cult, a direct offshoot of the earlier Christianized version of the Prophet Dance, made its appearance around 1860 or perhaps a bit earlier. The origin of this religious movement is usually ascribed to the prophet Smohalla who lived at the Wanapam village at Priest Rapids. Smohalla is said to have been killed in a fight, to have disappeared for a time, and when he again returned to his people to have said that he had been to the land of the dead. He told his people that some terrible natural catastrophe would destroy everything and then the Creator would restore the world as it was long ago. Only those who lead a good life could participate in the renewal of the world. The Smohalla cult, whose members were also called "Dreamers," preached the destruction of the whites and the sacredness of the earth. Special buildings were constructed in which to hold the religious services. Unlike the Traditional Prophet Dance, dancing was not emphasized and the ritual was more like a church service. Outdoor services involved the use of a special flag and marching around to the sound of a drum. The Smohalla cult was not a Christian religion; it simply made use of certain Christian ceremonial forms in its practice.

In the 1880's, at Mud Bay located on Puget Sound, another of these messianic religions was born. This religious movement, which came to be known as the Shakers, is still widely practiced. The traditional elements of the death of the messiah, visiting the land of the dead and receiving a message, then returning to life and spreading the message among a group of followers are all present in the Shaker religion. This religion was different in several ways, for while it preached leading a good life, it did not call for the disappearance of the whites. One of its primary emphases was the curing of the sick. Shaker churches may be found today at White Swan and Satus.

A variant form of the Prophet Dance movement, with distinct influence from the Smohalla cult and the Shaker church is the Pom Pom or feather religion, also called Washat. At the present time this is the most followed of the old religions on the Yakima reservation.

Many of the present day Yakima are followers of Protestant and Roman Catholic faiths.

The Yakima still adhere to many elements of their traditional beliefs. This may be seen in the existence of four Long Houses at Wapato, Satus, White Swan, and Toppenish. The Long Houses serve as the centers for carrying on the traditional ceremonial and religious life as well as for General Council meetings, educational and recreational activities and funerals.

Many modern marriages involve some of the elements of the traditional ceremonies.

Feasts are still held in the old pattern of the First Salmon Ceremony, or the ceremonies for the first roots and the first berries. Elements of the old economic patterns still survive. Some men will go to those traditional fishing localities that have not yet disappeared under the reservoir waters of a major hydro-electric dam to dipnet for salmon from the rickety platforms precariously suspended from the cliffs.

In late summer families will set up camps in

the mountains to gather berries and to hunt. Potato Hill near the foot of Mt. Adams is a favored place.

Some of the Yakima women carry on the traditional crafts of basket weaving and fashioning buckskin leather into attractive garments or moccasins.

THE YAKIMA OF TODAY AND TOMORROW

Although the Yakima people of today have clung tenaciously to many of the precious elements of the past, they are at the same time a vigorous and competitive part of today's world.

Tribal organization is based upon a General Council whose membership includes all members of the tribe over 18 years old, and 14 member Tribal Council whose members are elected for four year terms. The Tribal Council is empowered to transact the business affairs of the tribe, but matters of particular importance may be referred to the General Council.

The offices of the Tribal Council are located within the headquarters of the Agency and close liaison is maintained between these two organizations. The Tribal and Agency headquarters give the visitor the impression that he is visiting a large and busy corporation which, indeed, the Yakima Nation most certainly is. The Tribal Council carries on its business through a series of very busy committees. These are:

1. Timber, Grazing, Overall Economic Development.
2. Loan, Extension, Education, and Housing.
3. Roads, Irrigation and Land.
4. Legislative.
5. Fish, Wildlife, Law and Order.
6. Health, Employment, Welfare, Recreation and Youth Activities.
7. Enrollment.
8. Budget and Finance.

For many years the total number of Yakima people was not known because the allotment rolls were sadly out of date. Desiring to enroll all of the Yakima who were eligible, the general council sponsored federal legislation for enrollment of all members whether living on the reservation, on ceded lands, or elsewhere. The Act of August 9, 1946, established the minimum requirement for enrollment of one-fourth or more blood quantum of any of the 14 tribes or bands of the Yakima Nation. By July 1, 1971, the enrolled membership was 5,841, of which two-thirds lived on the reservation.

One of the major problems that has been facing the tribe is a result of the disastrous Allotment Act of 1887. This act provided for the allotment to individuals of tribally owned lands. Reluctantly the tribal members agreed to divide up the reservation. Each member was to receive 160 acres. It is reported that by 1914 when the rolls closed, 4,506 members had received allotments. Fee patents were granted to allottees and individuals were than free to disposed of their land. A great deal of land thus passed out of Yakima ownership.

Heirs to allotted land received fractionated ownership to the point where some pieces of land now have 120 owners. Only a third of the tracts are owned by individuals. It has been a tribal policy for some years to purchase these parcels of land from the Indian owners who wish to sell.

Much of the individually owned land is not farmed by the owner because of the small size of the tracts and the high cost of farm machinery and is, therefore, leased to others.

A substantial irrigation system has been developed over the years to serve the Indian and non-Indian farmers on and around the reservation. Nearly 150,000 acres of farm land are now under irrigation.

The keys to the future well being of the Yakima Nation are proper management and conservation of the rich resources of the reservation leading to full employment and economic security, and the education of the young people so that they will be able to compete successfully with their peers within the Indian community and in society at large.

Employment opportunities are improving on

CAMP CHAPARRAL Remedial Education summer camp.

Photograph by Harvey S. Rice, Washington Archaeological Research Center

the reservation. The lumber and wood products industries, the Yakima Agency, the Fort Simcoe Job Corps at White Swan, and the Wapato Irrigation Project offer many jobs. Another source of employment is agricultural labor, but much of this work is done by people of Mexican origin. A considerable amount of the on-reservation work is seasonal in nature, and many Yakima have moved off the reservation to find employment. The Tribal Council is working hard to attract new industry in order to improve the employment situation and raise the per capita income. To these ends, more than one million dollars of tribal funds have been invested in new industry.

Most of the tribal income comes from resources such as timber and grazing lands, or from payments obtained in claims for lost fishing rights or for lands taken without just compensation. Some of the Yakima lands are in individual allotments, and tribal members receive payment when these lands are logged. Annual per capita dividends from tribal income now amount to $300.00 per member.

To aid tribal members in securing either short-term or long-term loans, a Credit Program was established by the tribe in 1970. Members are now able to get money to finance housing, for agricultural purposes, and to establish new businesses or for other worthwhile purposes.

Housing has long been another tribal problem area. With many low income families on the reservation it was necessary to establish the Yakima Indian Tribal Housing Authority. The Housing Authority working with a number of existing programs has helped to provide much needed housing for many families. The Bureau of Indian Affairs has a number of aid and improvement programs to complement the programs of the Tribal Council.

The health needs of the Yakima are met primarily by the facilities operated by the Indian Health Service branch of the United States Public Health Service, by a contract hospital at Toppenish, and by contract health care by specialists. The Indian Health Service does not operate a hospital in this area. The Yakima people are dependent upon State and Federal health programs and, although health care has been improving rapidly in recent years, much remains to be done.

Community Action Programs are helping to meet many of the social needs. Through educational programs, counseling, and guidance individuals are being helped to help themselves.

The leaders of the Yakima Nation realize that through participation in educational programs of all kinds, on-the-job training, technical schools, colleges, and universities, the needs, the goals, and the aspirations of the Yakima people can be and will be met. The tribe budgets $100,000 annually for individual scholarships for their young people.

Nearly 1,700 students are currently enrolled in elementary through university academic training. In the magnificent forest lands of the mountain foothills in the western part of the reservation, a summer remedial education camp has been established. Known as Camp Chaparral, this facility hosts a number of groups throughout the summer and provides specially designed academic assistance programs for the younger students in grades three through nine.

Ever mindful of the need for economic improvement and an expanded educational base, the Yakima are nonetheless a proud, independent, and quietly aggressive people. They vigorously pursue their claims for lands unjustly taken and for fishing sites buried under the pools behind large dams across the Columbia River. They are equally vigorous in fighting attempts by State or Federal agencies to reinterpret the articles of the original treaty.

On July 8, 1972, a ceremony was held at the Toppenish Creek Ceremonial Grounds at White Swan to commemorate the return to the Yakima Nation of 21,000 acres of land on their sacred 12,000 foot high Mt. Adams.

The Yakima believe that the Creator put the mountain there as a monument to remind the Yakima that they are not the most important thing. The Creator provided in this way for the Yakima — the snow which gives life to everything.

On a clear day, Mt. Adams towers over all of Yakima territory. It stands there representing the ways of the past — the pursuit of game in the foothills and the gathering of wild plant foods on the lower slopes and the important watershed, and the meeting and trading with other tribes who were also attracted to the mountains.

Mt. Adams also symbolizes the present and the never-ending faith in the future. The Yakima still preserve much that is good from the past. They are still hunting the noble elk and other game and gathering food in the mountains, but modern paved highways take them to their accustomed places. As they travel they pass through their carefully managed forests where selective logging is providing them with economic security for generations to come. Most of all, Mt. Adams symbolizes the strength of the Yakima people who, in spite of years of adversity, have forged a truly strong and great Nation.

MOUNT ADAMS, the peak sacred to the Yakima people returned to
the sovereignty of the Yakima Indian nation in 1972 by President

chard M. Nixon.

STATEMENT OF THE CHAIRMAN
OF THE
YAKIMA TRIBAL COUNCIL

It has been my privilege for the past 16 years to serve on the Yakima Tribal Council since November, 1957, and to see many accomplishments. None has given me more concern or more pleasure than to participate in Claims Case 47-B. Two aspects of this experience have particularly pleased me. First, winning back in a precedent-setting decision Tract C including Mount Adams, through the efforts of our tribal claims attorney, Paul M. Niebell. Second, having the solid backing of the whole Tribe, with its strong desire to recover the land rather than to be paid for it. Without their support, the Tribal Council would never have been able to obtain the return to the Yakima people of Mount Adams.

The Mount Adams claim began in 1938. Paul M. Niebell is known in Washington, D. C. as an attorney's attorney. I have known many other attorneys who came to him for advice. His accomplishments for the Yakima people can be understood only from the viewpoint of a Yakima Indian, whose people once owned 11,000,000 acres of land by aboriginal title, and roamed through much more as far as the buffalo ranged and wherever the fish returned from the ocean in Washington, Montana, Idaho and Oregon, and who has retained his culture and religion. We feel that Mr. Niebell is responsible for maintaining our hunting and fishing rights — with over 100 cases protecting treaty fishing rights between 1966 and 1972 — winning a key water case in the Ahtanum Creek Treaty Water Rights case fought from 1908 to 1964. He won the battle in 1969 to stop Highway I-82, preventing the State of Washington and the U. S. Department of Justice from condemning Tribal Treaty Lands for an interstate highway.

98

Litigation for the recovery of Mount Adams began with passage of the Indian Claims Commission Act of August 13, 1946 (60 Stat. 1049). It continued from 1949 to 1972, to prove that an erroneous survey cannot give title to land. More important to Indians, the case proved that such a survey cannot take Treaty Land, which is not government or public land, but private property of the treaty signers — in this case the United States of America and the Yakima Indian Nation. The amount of Treaty Land returned to the Yakima Tribe, 21,008 acres, includes Mount Adams, a 12,000 foot high peak which is considered sacred by the Yakimas. It cannot be valued in dollars because it is *not for sale* at any price.

The return of this area cannot be mentioned without rendering due credit to the members of the tribal council: Harvey Adams, Louis Cloud, Moses Dick, Sr., Genevieve Hooper, Roger Jim, Johnson Meninick, William Northover, Joe Sampson, Mel Sampson, Eagle Seelatsee and Harris Teo, who stood wholeheartedly for the land return.

Delegates chosen by the Tribal Council to go to Washington, D. C. in 1972 when Mount Adams was returned were: Watson Totus, Johnson Meninick, Stanley Smartlowit, (deceased 1972) and Robert B. Jim, along with James B. Hovis, Tribal Attorney.

A public relations man in Washington, D. C., Mr. Jim Thomas (a Tlinget-Haida from Alaska) wrote hundreds of letters. He contacted Marlon Brando, who later became a committee of one who put us on the Today Show on Columbus Day in 1972. He also had Walter Cronkite show our side of the issue, and deserves much credit.

The Yakima people also received much help from Senators Henry M. Jackson, Warren Magnuson and Edward Kennedy, Representative Mike McCormack and many others. Don Wright, President of the Alaskan Federation of Natives, went to President Nixon twice on our behalf. The man who carried a personal load was Robert Robertson, aide to Vice-President Spiro Agnew. He must receive much credit for the return of Mount Adams through his contacts and consistent work along with Vice-President Agnew, who intervened for us with the President to obtain a long-awaited and welcome Executive Order.

On May 20, 1972, President Richard M. Nixon gave proof to my people that there is justice in America, and he restored a faith in a government that has long been mistrusted. Although we have not fared well in other claims or treaty matters, the President of the United States representing Indians as their trustee, in returning Mount Adams has shown the world the caliber leader he is. The Yakima Indian Nation is grateful.

The Yakima Tribal Council is pleased to make its struggles and accomplishments achieved with the help of the President and others mentioned above better known to the American people through Indian Tribal Series.

Robert B. Jim, Chairman
Yakima Tribal Council

100

SUGGESTED READING

These books represent studies by archae-
ologists, ethnologists, historians, and others who
have been particularly interested in the tribes of
the Plateau of Northwestern America. These are
reasonably accessible at major libraries.

AVERY MARY W. 1961. *History and Government of the State of Washington.* Seattle:
University of Washington Press.

Includes an excellent summary of the events
leading up to the signing of the treaty and the
war that followed.

BUTLER, B. ROBERT. 1965. *Perspectives on the
Prehistory of the Lower Columbia Valley.
Tebiwa: The Journal of the Idaho State
Museum. Vol. 8, No. 1, Pocatello.*

A preliminary statement based upon what was
known at that time.

CRESSMAN, LUTHER S. 1960. *Cultural Sequen-
ces at The Dalles, Oregon: A Contribution to
Pacific Northwest History.* Transaction of the
American Philosophical Society, New Series,
Vol. 50, Part 10.

A well illustrated report on 10,000 years of
culture history in this area of the Plateau.

DAUGHERTY, RICHARD D. 1956. *Archaeology of
the Lind Coulee Site, Washington.* Proceed-
ings of the American Philosophical Society,
Vol. 100, No. 3, pp. 223-78. Philadelphia.

Discussion of the excavation and discoveries

at the earliest archaeological site yet discovered in Washington.

DU BOIS, CORA. 1938. *The Feather Cult of the Middle Columbia.* General Series in Anthropology, No. 7 Menasha: George Banta Publishing Company.

A discussion of the origin and spread of this important religious movement.

MCWHORTER, LUCULLUS VIRGIL. 1913. *The Crime Against the Yakimas.* North Yakima, Wash: Republic Print.

Details the history of repressive legislation and deceit that has characterized this nation's dealings with the Yakima.

RAY, VERNE F. 1933. *The Sanpoil and Nespelem: Salishan People of Northeastern Washington.* University of Washington Publications in Anthropology, Vol. 5, University of Washington Press: Seattle.

An excellent ethnography of two northern Plateau groups.

RAY, VERNE F. 1939. *Cultural Relations in the Plateau of Northwestern America.* Los Angeles: The Southwest Museum.

A broad summary of the social and material culture of the Indian groups of the Plateau.

RELANDER, CLICK, ed. 1955. *The Yakima: Treaty Centennial, 1855-1955.* Yakima: The Republic Press.

A brief history of the Yakima.

———————— 1956. *Drummers and Dreamers.* Caxton Printers, Ltd. Caldwell, Idaho.

The story of the prophet Smohalla and of his nephew Puck Hyah Toot and of the Wanapam people living at Priest Rapids on the Columbia River.

SPLAWN, ANDREW JACKSON. 1917. *Ka-mi-akin, the Last Hero of the Yakimas.* Portland: Kilham Stationery and Print Co.

A sympathetic treatment of the Indian side of the war of 1855-59.

SPIER, LESLIE. 1935. *The Prophet Dance of the Northwest and its Derivatives: the Source of the Ghost Dance.* General Series in Anthropology, No. 1 Menasha: George Banta Publishing Company.

A discussion of the origins and spread of prophet type religions in the western United States.

SPIER, LESLIE AND EDWARD SAPIR. 1930. *Wishram Ethnography.* University of Washington Publications in Anthropology, Vol. 3, No. 3, pp. 151-300. University of Washington Press.

An excellent descriptive anthropological study.

RICHARD D. DAUGHERTY is Professor of Anthropology and Director of the Washington Archaeological Research Center at Washington State University. A native of the State of Washington, Daugherty earned his B.A. and Ph.D. degrees at the University of Washington. Daugherty has conducted archaeological work in Egypt, Sudan, France, and Spain, but his primary interest has always been in the prehistoric cultures of the Pacific Northwest. He was appointed by President Lyndon B. Johnson to The Advisory Council on Historic Preservation. By resolution the State Senate has designated Daugherty to be "A Distinguished Citizen of the State of Washington."